Homemade Bath and Shower Products

DIY All-Natural Bath Salts, Bath Milks, Bath Bombs, Shower Gels, Bubble Baths, Bath Teas, Body Scrubs and Suds

Josephine Simon

Copyrights

All rights reserved. © Josephine Simon and Maplewood Publishing No part of this publication or the information in it may be quoted from or reproduced in any form by means such as printing, scanning, photocopying, or otherwise without prior written permission of the copyright holder.

Disclaimer and Terms of Use

Effort has been made to ensure that the information in this book is accurate and complete. However, the author and the publisher do not warrant the accuracy of the information, text, and graphics contained within the book due to the rapidly changing nature of science, research, known and unknown facts, and internet. The author and the publisher do not hold any responsibility for errors, omissions, or contrary interpretation of the subject matter herein. This book is presented solely for motivational and informational purposes only. The publisher and author of this book does not control or direct users' actions and are not responsible for the information or content shared, harm and/or action of the book readers. The presentation of the information is without contract or any type of guarantee assurance. This book is not meant to be used, nor should it be used, to diagnose or treat any medical condition. For diagnosis or treatment of any medical problem, consult your own physician. The publisher and author are not responsible for any specific health or allergy needs that may require medical supervision and are not liable for any damages or negative consequences from any treatment, action, application or preparation, to any person reading or following the information in this book. References, if any, are provided for informational purposes only and do not constitute endorsement of any websites or other sources. Readers should be aware that the websites listed in this book, if any, may change.

ISBN: 978-1542539340

Printed in the United States

Avant-Propos

Have you been thinking to yourself that you would really like to try your hand at creating your own natural bath products? Or have you been approaching the gift giving season looking for ways to bring natural homemade beauty into the lives of your friends and loved ones? If either of these describes you, then this book of natural homemade bath products is a dream come true. It's incredibly easy to create your own bath salts, bath teas, fizzies, scrubs, and more. What makes this even better is that each ingredient in this book is all natural, with no chemical names that you cannot pronounce, let alone really know what they are. The formulas here are luxurious and sophisticated; however, they are so simple to make that even a young child can help. This book is the perfect introduction, or complement, to a lifestyle that focuses on natural health and natural beauty.

Contents

Introduction 1
   Glossary of Common Ingredients 3
Bath Salts 8
   Peace, Love and Joy Bath Salts 10
   Banish the Blues Bath Salts 12
   Time to Pause Bath Salts 14
   Vanilla Almond Bath Salts 16
   Spice of Life Bath Salts 18
   Sore Muscle Relief Bath Salts 20
   Warm and Woodsy Bath Salts 22
Powdered Milk Baths 24
   Warm Milk Before Bed Nighttime Bath Powder 26
   Skin Soothing Gentle Milk Bath 27
   Exotic Floral Milk Bath 28
   Cinnamon Vanilla Steamed Milk Bath 29
   Lavender Peppermint Sinus and Headache Soothing Milk Bath 30
   Orange Cream Milk Bath 32
   Love is in the Air Milky Bath 34
Bath Bombs 36
   Bubbly Spirit Bath Bombs 38
   Holiday Stress Relief Bath Bombs 40
   Muscle Melt Bath Bombs 42
   Spiced Vanilla Mega Bombs 44
   Clarity and Wisdom Energizing Mega Bombs 45
   Fatigue Busting Mega Bombs 46
   Tropical Paradise Bath Bombs 47
   Coming Up Roses Bath Bombs 48
   Sweet Relief Bath Bombs 49
Shower Gels and Body Cleansers 50
   Unscented Moisturizing Shower Gel 52
   Lavender Cocoa Butter Cleanser 53
   Delicate Orange Blossom Milky Gel 54

- Rosemary and Tea Tree Aloe Shower Gel 56
- Green Tea and Lemon Essence Shower Gel 58
- Vanilla Milk and Honey Shower Gel 60
- Bees Knees Citrus Honey Wash 61

Bubbly Baths 62
- Vanilla Rose Silky Bubble Bath 64
- Rosemary Lavender Foaming Bath Tonic 65
- Extra Foamy Vanilla Nutmeg Bubble Bath 66
- Lemon Eucalyptus Bubbly Honey Bath 67
- Sniffles Be Gone Bath Suds 68
- Jasmine Scented Bubbly 69
- Just For Him Relaxing Bubble Bath 70
- Baby Your Baby Gentle Bubble Bath 71
- Energizing Citrus Bubbly 72

Bath Teas 74
- Ultra Soothing Chamomile Lavender Bath Tea 76
- Antioxidant Bath Tea 77
- Chai Bath Tea 78
- Sniffle Relief Bath Tea 79
- Cypress Lime Bath Tea 80
- Brighten Up Buttercup Bath Tea 81
- Hop To It Bath Tea 82

Body Scrubs and Suds 84
- Smooth as Silk Body Scrub 86
- Honey Almond Brown Sugar Scrub 87
- Masculine Dead Sea Scrub 88
- Skin Brightening Coffee Scrub 89
- Rosemary Lemon Salt Scrub 90
- Luscious Lemon Lime Sugar Scrub 91
- Sweet Peppermint Scrub 92
- Cedar Rose Moisturizing Body Wash 93
- Tea Tree and Honey Restorative Body Wash 94
- Milky Chamomile Wash 95

Conclusion 96
More Books from Josephine Simon 98

Introduction

Some of life's best indulgences happen in the bathtub. Here is where we allow ourselves to unwind and forget about life for just a few minutes. In the warm waters of a bath, we recharge ourselves and renew our spirits. You work hard, and your body and spirit need a little pampering. Luxurious bath products are one way you can treat yourself with little decadence – without guilt.

Maybe you head to your local specialty boutique, or the aisles of your neighborhood drug store, looking for just the right product. Not finding what you want, you take your search online to look for bath products that nourish your skin and restore your spirit, but the more you look, the more you realize that many of the bath and body products we have grown to enjoy and rely upon are filled with chemicals that you can't even pronounce. Why would you want to sit in a bathtub filled with all of that? The good news is that natural bath products are easy to make right in your own home and require very little in terms of investment of your time or money.

Not only can you make all-natural bath products for yourself, but every recipe included in this book makes a wonderful gift as well. You can show the people in your life just how much you care about them by creating for them a moment of luxury that is natural, wholesome, and safe. Within this book you will find recipes for a variety of body scrubs, bath salts, bath milk, bath teas, and even the ever popular bath fizzies. There is without question something here for everyone, including masculine scents and formulas created for those with the most sensitive skin.

The true beauty of natural bath products is that you have the ability to tailor them to your needs. In most cases, substitutions can be made without altering the product too much. Here are just a few things to consider when making substitutions in your homemade bath products.

- If you don't care for the scent of an essential oil, by all means feel free to substitute another oil. Just keep in mind that some oils might be irritating to the skin, so never add more than the suggested amount of any essential oil to the formula. It is also always wise to do a skin test with 1-3 drops of essential oil diluted in a carrier oil. Apply it to your skin and check for any reaction over the next 12-24 hours.
- Also make note that most essential oils have suggested therapeutic properties and you might want to take that into consideration when changing out the scents. For example, if you are looking for a soothing and relaxing scent, you will want to stay away from energizing essential oils, such as those belonging to the citrus family.
- For formulas that call for carrier or other oils, feel free to exchange for your oil of preference. Just keep in mind that different oils have different viscosity, color, and aroma. These characteristics can alter the final product slightly.
- When making body scrubs, you can easily interchange salt, white sugar, or brown sugar.
- Types of powdered milk are interchangeable in recipes that call for it. If you prefer a nut-based milk powder, coconut milk powder is a good alternative.

When you craft natural homemade bath products, you are creating them with love and pure intentions. To carry through with the spirit of natural products, try to choose ingredients that are of the best quality you can afford. When possible, choose organic and locally sourced ingredients, such as locally farmed honey.

Crafting your own bath products is actually very simple. You might think you need to go out and break the bank buying special supplies and containers. The truth is that you probably already have most of what you need in your pantry. To help you along the way in creating your own natural bath products for yourself or for gifts, we have included a glossary of some of the most common natural bath products:

Glossary of Common Ingredients

Absolutes: Fragrance absolutes are similar to essential oils in the fact that they are oily essences that are extracted directly from the plant. The main difference between an essential oil and an absolute is that essential oils are generally extracted via steam distillation, while absolutes use a solvent to help extract the oils. Once the extraction has occurred, the solution is filtered; however, a small amount of the solvent may be left behind in the final product. So, although absolutes are similar to, if not stronger than, essential oils in terms of scent, they are not technically as pure. For this reason, absolutes are used more as fragrance agents than for therapeutic purposes. Common absolutes you will find are vanilla, rose, and orange blossom.

Baking soda: Sodium bicarbonate, or baking soda, is not just for baking. This powdery kitchen staple has a multitude of health and beauty uses! It can be used as an exfoliant, antiseptic, antifungal, skin softener, cleanser, and deodorant. Baking soda can be added to natural bath products for additional natural healing properties and to improve the texture.

Buttermilk powder: This product is created by dehydrating buttermilk until all the moisture has been removed. It can take the place of standard powdered milk in any bath product recipe. The purpose of buttermilk powder is similar to that of powdered milk – it acts as a powder base and works to soothe and soften the skin. Buttermilk is more acidic than cow's milk, and therefore has increased exfoliating properties.

Citric Acid: Citric acid is a naturally occurring alkalizing agent that is often used in foods to preserve taste, color, and texture. In health and beauty products it takes on a different role. Citric acid is a beneficial exfoliating agent and helps to keep the pH levels of your skin balanced. Citric acid is often used in bath bombs because it helps to create the fizzing, bubbling effect that is often desired from these products.

Coconut Milk Powder: Similar in function and consistency to cow's milk powder, coconut milk powder adds soothing and moisturizing properties to natural bath products. Coconut milk can result in a slightly creamier product, and it has a delicate coconut scent.

Cornstarch: Cornstarch is another kitchen staple that can take on new life as a natural beauty ingredient. The texture of cornstarch is smooth and slippery, which makes it the perfect base for body powders or as an additive to milk baths and bath bombs. Cornstarch is soothing to irritated skin, and it has antifungal properties.

Dried flowers and herbs: You will find that many natural bath products use dried flowers and herbs. Sometimes larger pieces are used, while other times they are ground into a fine powder. Dried flowers and herbs are intact, natural plants that have been dried until no moisture remains. They still contain the nutritive qualities of the plant, as well as the same fragrance and flavor. Dried flowers and herbs are generally more concentrated ounce for ounce than their fresh counterparts. Dried flowers and herbs do not dissolve in water, so if having them float around or stick to your body is not desirable for you, you can either strain the finished product through cheesecloth or a large tea bag, or you can grind them up so finely that they disperse more evenly, and are less noticeable in the water.

Epsom salt: Magnesium sulfate, or Epsom salt, is a pure mineral compound in crystallized form. It is not the same as table salt or sea salt. Epsom salt is used primarily for health and beauty purposes, with one of its most well-known uses being its ability to soothe and relax sore and tired muscles. Epsom salt is added to bath salts and body scrubs and helps to soothe the skin, release stress from muscles, and exfoliate. It is possible that some of the magnesium is absorbed through the skin and can help alleviate common magnesium deficiency.

Essential oils: Essential oils are the pure oily essences of plants and flowers. Essential oils are generally steam distilled and can be extracted from the plants' leaves, roots, stems, and petals. Essential oils are pure, highly concentrated substances and should be treated as therapeutic grade agents. Most essential oils need to be diluted before being applied to the skin, and a little bit goes a long way. For natural bath purposes, essential oils are used as both fragrance agents and for their therapeutic properties.

Goat's Milk Powder: Just like cow's milk powder, buttermilk powder, and coconut milk powder, goat's milk powder is the resulting product of dehydrating liquid goat milk until a powder consistency is achieved. It can be used as a base for bath milks and as an additive for bath salts, body cleansers, and bath bombs. Goat milk powder is high in vitamin A, vitamin B, vitamin E, and beta carotene. It nourishes and softens the skin. Goat's milk powder is excellent for gentle exfoliation and for maintaining moisture.

Honey: Raw honey is one of nature's marvels. It has antibacterial properties, and acts as an antioxidant for your skin. It also soothes and acts as a humectant, which helps to retain moisture. It can also be used as an exfoliant, and in the bath to rejuvenate and refresh your whole body. It's always best to use local honey if possible.

Aloe Vera Gel: This is the gel-like substance that is extracted from the leaves of the aloe vera plant. You can find all natural, pure aloe vera gel or formulations with other ingredients added. For the purpose of creating natural bath products, you will want to go with the purest form you can find. Aloe vera gel works to soothe and heal irritated skin, provides a moisture barrier, and it makes a nice base for certain gel-based body products. The scent is very light and can easily be masked.

Oatmeal/Oat Flour: Using oatmeal or ground oats in bath products lends a soothing property that is especially good for dry, irritated, and chapped skin. It also leaves behind a slightly milky residue which will helps seal moisture into the skin.

Powdered Milk: Made from dehydrated cow's milk, powdered milk makes a great soothing base for milk baths and creamy cleansers. It can also be used with cornstarch as a soothing, healing powder. Powdered milk is best used for its soothing and softening properties.

Sea Salt: Sea salt is a coarse grain salt that has several useful properties for health and beauty products. Sea salt has a high mineral content which helps to nourish the skin. It also works as a softener, an exfoliation agent, and an antibacterial.

Therapeutic grade clay: There are several kinds of medicinal mineral clay. Types that can be used in health and beauty products include kaolin clay, bentonite clay, and fuller's earth clay. Clay is used in bath products to balance the skin, heal irritated skin, and to soften. Depending on the amount of clay used, a residue may remain on the body. Because clay can be overly drying when left on the skin for long periods of time, it is advised that you quickly shower off after soaking in a healing clay preparation.

Bath Salts

Bath salts are magical crystals that infuse your bath with luscious fragrance and therapeutic oils while relaxing every muscle of your body. The combination of Epsom salt and other therapeutic ingredients creates a whole body relaxation spa treatment. These bath salts are easy to mix and only need to sit for a few days to allow the scents of the essential oils to infuse the mixture. Special gifting suggestions have been included to make these bath salts even more memorable and unique.

Peace, Love and Joy Bath Salts

Materials:
2 cups Epsom salt
1 ½ cups sea salt
½ cup baking soda
10 drops vanilla absolute
10 drops jasmine essential oil
10 drops bergamot essential oil
Jars with tightly fitted lids

Instructions:
1. In a large bowl, combine the Epsom salt, sea salt, and baking soda. Use a fork or whisk to blend the dry ingredients.
2. In a small glass container, combine the vanilla absolute, jasmine essential oil, and bergamot essential oil.
3. Sprinkle the combined oils over the dry ingredients.
4. Use the fork to blend in the oils, taking extra care to break up any small clumps that form.
5. Transfer the bath salt to jars and fill them approximately three-quarters of the way full.
6. Place the lids on the jars, tightly seal them, and store in a cool, dry place for 3-5 days.
7. Shake the jars vigorously to redistribute the oils, which may have settled.

To Use:
1. Add a ½ cup to warm bath water and allow the salt to dissolve before entering the bath.
2. Soak for twenty minutes and enjoy.

Suggestions for Gifting:
1. Once the dry ingredients have been blended, divide the mixture up into three separate smaller bowls. Rather than combine the three oils together, add one oil to each of the powder portions and blend. Use natural food coloring to add a light tint to each portion, if desired.
2. Place each portion in its own separate tightly lidded jar for three to five days, and then shake vigorously.
3. Transfer the bath salts in layers into shallow, wide mouth gifting jars. Include a description of each layer and instructions to use a spoon to scoop out a combination of the three layers when adding the salts to the bath water.

Banish the Blues Bath Salts

Materials:
2 cups pink Himalayan sea salt
1 cup Epsom salt
½ cup baking soda
15 drops tangerine essential oil
15 drops rosemary essential oil
1 teaspoon orange zest
Jars with tightly fitted lids

Instructions:
1. In a large bowl, combine the pink Himalayan sea salt, Epsom salt, and baking soda. Use a fork or whisk to blend until the mixture is well combined.
2. Sprinkle the tangerine and rosemary essential oils over the dry mixture.
3. Use a fork to blend, taking care to break up any clumps that may form.
4. Once the mixture is well blended, add the orange zest and mix again.
5. Transfer the mixture to jars, filling each one approximately three-quarters of the way full.
6. Place the lids on the jars and store them in a cool, dry place for at least 3-5 days.
7. Shake each jar vigorously before using.

To Use:
1. Add a ½ cup to warm bath water and swirl with your hand to dissolve. If you do not like the orange zest floating in the bath water, simply wrap the ½ cup of bath salts in a piece of cheesecloth, form a pouch, and tie it securely shut. Place the pouch in the bath water and steep.
2. Soak for 15-20 minutes and enjoy.

Suggestions for Gifting:
1. Place a sprig of fresh rosemary in each jar for an additional decorative touch. Also include cheesecloth or muslin pouches to steep the bath salts in.

Time to Pause Bath Salts

Materials:
2 cups Epsom salt
1 cup Dead Sea salt
½ cup green clay powder
½ cup baking soda
20 drops lavender essential oil
5 drops sandalwood essential oil
5 drops frankincense essential oil
¼ cup dried lavender flowers, finely ground
Jars with tightly fitted lids

Instructions:
1. Combine the Epsom salt, Dead Sea salt, green clay powder and baking soda together in a large bowl.
2. Using a fork or a whisk, blend the dry ingredients together until they are thoroughly combined.
3. In a small glass container, combine the lavender essential oil, sandalwood essential oil, and frankincense essential oil. Mix well.
4. Sprinkle the oil mixture over the dry ingredients.
5. Use a fork to mix and incorporate the oils, taking care to break up any clumps that may form.
6. Once mixed, add the finely ground lavender flowers and mix again.
7. Transfer the mixture to jars and fill them approximately three-quarters of the way full.
8. Place the lid on the jars and store them in a cool, dry place for at least 3-5 days.
9. Shake the jars vigorously before the first use to distribute the oils.

To Use:
1. Place a ½ cup of the mixture in warm bath water and dissolve.
2. Soak for 15-20 minutes and enjoy. When you are finished with your bath, rinse off under a quick shower, if desired, to remove any residue from the clay.

Suggestions for Gifting:
1. Make a relaxing eye mask to go along with the bath salt. Sew together a pouch measuring approximately 3"x6" out of cotton or another gentle fabric. Combine 1 ½ cups uncooked white rice, 1 tablespoon fresh herbs like basil, lavender, or rosemary. Add 10-12 drops of your favorite essential oil. Mix well Transfer the rice mixture to a baking sheet and place in the pre-heated oven at 350°F and bake for 15 minutes. Let the infused rice cool down and transfer to the pouch and sew it shut. The rice mask can be placed in the microwave for 30 seconds or in the freezer for one hour before using.

Vanilla Almond Bath Salts

Materials:
2 cups Epsom salt
1 cup sea salt
½ cup baking soda
¼ cup almond flour
20 drops vanilla absolute
15 drops Roman chamomile essential oil
Jars with tightly fitted lids

Instructions:
1. In a large bowl, combine the Epsom salt, sea salt, baking soda, and almond flour. Use a fork or a whisk to mix the dry ingredients until they are well blended.
2. Sprinkle the vanilla absolute and roman chamomile essential oil over the dry ingredients.
3. Use a fork to blend the oils into the dry mixture, taking care to break up any clumps that may form.
4. Transfer the mixture to the jars, filling each approximately three-quarters of the way full.
5. Seal the jars and store them in a cool, dry place for at least 3-5 days.
6. Shake each jar vigorously before the first use to help distribute the oils.

To Use:
1. Add a ½ cup to warm bath water and allow to the mixture to dissolve.
2. Soak for 15-20 minutes and enjoy.

Suggestions for Gifting:
1. Attach a small wooden scoop to the outside of each jar as a useful decorative addition. Also include a natural vanilla scented candle that can be enjoyed at the same time as the bath salts.

Spice of Life Bath Salts

Materials:
2 cups Epson salt
1 cup Dead Sea salt
½ cup baking soda
10 drops ginger essential oil
10 drops lemongrass essential oil
5 drops thyme essential oil
5 drops rosemary essential oil
Jars with tightly fitted lids

Instructions:
1. In a large bowl, combine the Epsom salt, Dead Sea salt, and baking soda. Use a whisk or a fork to mix the dry ingredients together.
2. In a small glass container, combine the ginger essential oil, lemongrass essential oil, thyme essential oil and rosemary essential oil. Swirl to blend.
3. Sprinkle the essential oil blend over the dry ingredients.
4. Use a fork to blend the oils into the salt mixture, taking care to break up any clumps that may form.
5. Transfer the mixture into glass jars, filling them each approximately three-quarters of the way full.
6. Cover the jars tightly and store them in a cool, dark place for at least 3-5 days.
7. Shake the jars vigorously to distribute the essential oils before using for the first time.

To Use:
1. Add a ½ cup of the bath salts to warm bath water and allow them to dissolve.
2. Soak for 15-20 minutes and enjoy.

Suggestions for Gifting:
1. Pair this blend with a natural bristle bath brush or loofah, along with instructions to brush the body in circular motions moving up towards the heart.

Sore Muscle Relief Bath Salts

Materials:
2 cups Epsom salt
1 cup sea salt
½ cup baking soda
10 drops eucalyptus essential oil
10 drops rosemary essential oil
10 drops lavender essential oil
Jars with tightly fitted lids

Instructions:
1. In a large bowl, combine the Epsom salt, sea salt, and baking soda. Use a fork or a whisk to thoroughly blend the mixture.
2. Sprinkle each of the oils over the salt mixture.
3. Once all of the essential oils have been added, mix the salts with a fork to thoroughly blend in the oils. Take care to break up any clumps that may form.
4. Transfer the salts to glass jars, filling each approximately three-quarters of the way full.
5. Tightly seal the jars and store them in a cool, dry place for at least 3-4 days.
6. Shake each jar vigorously before the first use to evenly distribute the essential oils.

To Use:
1. Add ½ to 1 cup of the bath salts to a warm or hot bath. Swirl the water to dissolve.
2. Soak for 15-20 minutes, or until relief is felt.

Suggestions for Gifting:
1. Add a sprig of rosemary or dry eucalyptus to the outside of the gifting jar as a decorative accent. You can also add same kind and amount of the included essential oils into 1-2 ounces of almond oil to create a soothing muscle massage oil to gift along with the bath salts.

Warm and Woodsy Bath Salts

Materials:
3 cups Epsom salt
½ cup baking soda
10 drops sandalwood essential oil
10 drops patchouli essential oil
5 drops thyme essential oil
5 drops vetiver essential oil
Glass jars with tightly fitted lids

Instructions:
1. In a large bowl, mix together the Epsom salt and baking soda.
2. In a small glass container, mix together the sandalwood, patchouli, thyme, and vetiver essential oils. Swirl to mix.
3. Sprinkle the essential oil mixture over the salt. Using a fork, blend the oils into the salt, taking care to break up any clumps that may form.
4. Transfer the salt to glass jars, filling each approximately three-quarters of the way full.
5. Tightly seal the jars and store them in a cool, dry place for at least 3-5 days.
6. Shake the jars vigorously before using the first time to help distribute the essential oils.

To Use:
1. Pour a ½ cup under warm running bath water and allow the salts to dissolve.
2. Soak for 15-20 minutes and enjoy.

Suggestions for Gifting:
1. This scent is unisex and perfect for the man on your gift list. To make the salts more visually appealing, try brewing half a cup of very strong black tea and allowing it to cool. When you are preparing the bath salts, sprinkle the tea onto the salt, while mixing, adding just enough to give it a little bit of color. Spread the salt out on a parchment-lined baking sheet and allow it to dry. Break up any clumps before transferring it to the jars. For an extra warming scent, try adding a couple of whole cloves into the bottom of each gifting jar before adding the salts.

Powdered Milk Baths

Creamy milk baths are the ultimate treat for soothing and softening skin. A variety of powdered milks can be used, such as powdered cow's milk, powdered goat's milk, and powdered buttermilk. Any type of powdered milk can be substituted into any of these recipes, including powdered coconut milk. Special gifting suggestions have been included in case you choose to share the decadence of these milk baths with others.

Warm Milk Before Bed Nighttime Bath Powder

Materials:
2 cups powdered milk
1 cup powdered goat's milk
1 cup Epsom salt
20 drops lavender essential oil
10 drops chamomile essential oil
Glass jars with tight lids
Blender

Instructions:
1. Place the powdered milk, powdered goat's milk, and Epsom salt in a blender. Pulse quickly to combine and slightly break down the Epsom salt.
2. Add the essential oils to the mix, working in two to three increments, blending briefly after each addition.
3. Transfer the powder to glass jars with tight fitting lids.
4. Store in a cool, dry place.

To Use:
1. Add ½ to 1 cup of the milk bath to warm bath water in the evening.
2. Soak for 15-20 minutes and enjoy.

Suggestions for Gifting
1. Place the powder in a decorative plastic bag and secure it shut with a tight twist tie. Place the bag inside a large mug, preferably one that looks suitable for enjoying warm nighttime milk in. Write the instructions for use on a small card decorated with the nighttime sky.

Skin Soothing Gentle Milk Bath

Materials:
2 cups powdered goat's milk
2 cups powdered milk
½ cup cornstarch
½ cup baking soda
Glass jars with tight fitting lids

Instructions:
1. Combine the powdered goat's milk, powdered milk, cornstarch, and baking soda in a large bowl.
2. Whisk the powders together until thoroughly combined.
3. Transfer the milk bath powder to jars with tightly fitting lids.
4. Store in a cool, dry place.

To Use:
1. Add ½ to 1 cup of the milk bath to lukewarm bath water and let the milk bath dissolve.
2. Soak for 15-20 minutes and enjoy. Gently pat your skin dry when you are finished.

Suggestions for Gifting;
1. Powdered goat's milk can have a scent that is undesirable to some people. If you are gifting this milk bath, try adding up to 10-15 drops of a gentle, non-irritating essential oil to help mask the smell. Chamomile or lavender essential oils are mild in scent, soothing to the skin, and generally well tolerated.

Exotic Floral Milk Bath

Materials:
2 cups powdered milk
¼ cup rice flour
¼ cup dried jasmine petals, ground (can use jasmine tea instead, if desired)
10 drops jasmine essential oil
10 drops ylang ylang essential oil
5 drops rose absolute
Glass jars with tight fitting lids
Blender

Instructions:
1. In a blender, combine the powdered milk, rice flour, and jasmine petals or jasmine tea. Pulse quickly, just until the jasmine is ground into the powder.
2. Add the jasmine essential oil, ylang ylang essential oil, and rose absolute. Quickly pulse to incorporate the oils throughout the powder.
3. Transfer the powder to glass jars and cover tightly.
4. Let the powder sit for at least 24 hours and then shake or stir vigorously to ensure the oils are blended throughout.
5. Store in a cool, dry place.

To Use:
1. Add approximately ½ cup to warm bath water and allow the mixture to dissolve.
2. Soak for 15-20 minutes and enjoy.

Suggestions for Gifting:
1. Place this milk bath in a beautiful decorative jar and gift along with a bouquet of the recipient's favorite exotic flowers.

Cinnamon Vanilla Steamed Milk Bath

Materials:
2 cups powdered milk
½ cup cornstarch
¼ cup red or pink therapeutic grade powdered clay
2 teaspoons ground cinnamon
15 drops vanilla absolute
Jar with tightly fitting lid

Instructions:
1. In a large bowl, combine the powdered milk, cornstarch, therapeutic grade powdered clay, and cinnamon. Whisk together until thoroughly blended.
2. Add the vanilla absolute and whisk again, blending in the vanilla absolute as thoroughly as possible.
3. Transfer the milk bath to a glass jar and cover tightly.
4. Let the milk bath sit for at least 24 hours. Stir or shake the mixture to ensure that the scent is evenly distributed.
5. Store in a cool, dry place.

To Use:
1. Add a ¼ to ½ cup of the mixture to comfortably hot bath water and allow it to dissolve.
2. Soak for 15-20 minutes and enjoy.

Suggestions for Gifting:
1. This creation is all about warmth and decadence. Place this mixture in clear glass jar with a wooden lid and gift it with a homemade treat, crafted from the finest and purest ingredients in your kitchen. Vanilla scented caramels or a homemade chai tea blend are nice accompaniments to this richly scented bath.

Lavender Peppermint Sinus and Headache Soothing Milk Bath

Materials:
2 ½ cups powdered milk
½ cup baking soda
2 tablespoons dried lavender flowers
1 tablespoon dried peppermint leaves
20 drops lavender essential oil
10 drops peppermint essential oil
Jars with tight fitting lids
Spice or coffee grinder

Instructions:
1. In a bowl, combine the powdered milk and baking soda.
2. Place the dried lavender flowers and the dried peppermint leaves in a spice or coffee grinder and pulse until the mixture is powdery.
3. Add the ground lavender and peppermint to the milk mixture.
4. Sprinkle in the lavender and peppermint essential oils. Use a fork or a whisk to incorporate the oils throughout the milk. Take care to break up any clumps that may form.
5. Transfer the milk powder to jars and close tightly.
6. Store in a cool, dry place.

To Use:
1. Add a ½ cup to 1 cup of the milk bath to warm bath water. Swirl the water with your hands to dissolve the mixture.
2. Soak for 15-20 minutes and enjoy.

Suggestions for Gifting:
1. An old fashioned milk bottle makes an attractive container for milk baths. Make this headache formula a little extra pretty by tying a small dried lavender bouquet to the bottle with a piece of twine. The scent from the lavender will infuse the room it is in, which helps to encourage relaxation and release stress.

Orange Cream Milk Bath

Materials:
2 ½ cups powdered milk
½ cup cornstarch
¼ cup almond flour, finely ground
15 drops sweet orange essential oil
10 drops vanilla absolute
Jars with tight fitting lids

Instructions:
1. Combine the powdered milk, cornstarch, and almond flour together in a large bowl.
2. Sprinkle on the sweet orange essential oil and the vanilla absolute. Use a fork or a whisk to blend the mixture until the oils are distributed throughout.
3. Transfer the mixture to glass jars, filling them approximately three-quarters of the way full.
4. Cover, and let sit for at least 24 hours.
5. Shake the mixture vigorously before the first use to ensure that the oils are distributed.
6. Store in a cool, dry place.

To Use:
1. Pour a ¼ to ½ cup under warm running bath water. Allow the milk mixture to dissolve.
2. Soak for 15-20 minutes and enjoy.

Suggestions for Gifting:
1. Make this energizing and moisturizing formula extra special by adding a teaspoon of orange zest to the powdered milk. When transferring it to decorative gift jars or bottles, add a small, whole vanilla bean to the center. Gift the milk bath with a large reusable tea bag to place it in so the oils from the orange zest can be released without needing to clean the orange zest from the bathtub.

Love is in the Air Milky Bath

Materials:
2 cups powdered milk
1 cup powdered coconut milk
½ cup cornstarch
10 drops patchouli essential oil
10 drops jasmine essential oil
5 drops ylang ylang essential oil
5 drops vanilla absolute
Jars with tight fitting lids

Instructions:
1. Combine the powdered milk, powdered coconut milk, and cornstarch in a large bowl.
2. Sprinkle the patchouli essential oil, jasmine essential oil, ylang ylang essential oil and vanilla absolute over the powdery mixture.
3. Use a fork or a whisk to blend the oils into the milk. Take care to break up any small clumps that may form.
4. Transfer the mixture to a jar, filling it approximately ¾ of the way full.
5. Cover and let sit for at least 24 hours.
6. Shake the jar vigorously before the first use to make sure that the essential oils are distributed throughout.
7. Store in a cool, dry place.

To Use:
1. Add ¼ - ½ cup of the milk bath to a warm bath. Swirl the water with your hand to help the milk bath dissolve.
2. Soak for 15-20 minutes and enjoy.

Suggestions for Gifting:
1. Add a little bit of natural red or pink food coloring to the milk mixture when you add in the oils. Also, add a tablespoon of dried, coarsely ground rose petals to the milk bath before placing in the jar.

Bath Bombs

Bath bombs, or bath fizzies, are therapeutic nuggets of joy. Just drop one or two of these, depending on their size, into your bath water and you instantly transform your bathing experience. Bath bombs are easy to make. All you need is a few ingredients and some type of mold, such as one specially designed for making bath bombs. You can also use candy molds, ice cube trays and soap molds. If you like a more rustic approach, you can simply form them with your hands. Smaller molds will require that you add 2 bath bombs to each bath while one larger mold will be sufficient for a single bath. If you are gifting these bath bombs you can get creative by adding natural food colorings, using novelty molds or piping them into mini cupcake liners using a pastry bag with decorative tips. You can gift bath bombs in any type of packaging, but for long term storage they should be kept in a sealed, air tight container.

Bubbly Spirit Bath Bombs

Materials:
1 cup baking soda
½ cup Epsom salt
½ cup citric acid
1 tablespoon sweet almond oil
10 drops ginger essential oil
10 drops grapefruit essential oil
10 drops peppermint essential oil
Water for misting
Appropriate mold

Instructions:
1. Combine the baking soda, Epson salt and citric acid in a large bowl. Use a whisk or a fork to combine the mixture.
2. Next, add in the almond oil and sprinkle in the grapefruit essential oil, grapefruit essential oil and peppermint essential oil. Use a fork or a whisk to blend the mixture, taking care to break up any clumps that form from the oil.
3. Once the mixture is blended, begin misting it lightly with water while continuing to whisk it. Blend until the mixture is damp enough that when you form a ball with it in your hands it maintains it shape.
4. Firmly press the mixture into the molds that you are using.
5. Set the molds out on the counter and let them sit for 24 hours.
6. Remove the bath bombs from the mold and let them air dry for at least 24 hours.
7. Store them in a tightly covered container until ready to use.

To Use:
1. Place one large or two small bath bombs into warm bath water.
2. Soak for 15-20 minutes and enjoy.

Holiday Stress Relief Bath Bombs

Materials:
1 cup baking soda
½ cup Epsom salt
½ cup citric acid
1 tablespoon coconut oil, melted
10 drops peppermint essential oil
10 drops frankincense essential oil
5 drops sweet orange essential oil
Water for misting
Appropriate molds
Natural red or green food coloring, optional

Instructions:
1. Combine the baking soda, Epson salt and citric acid in a large bowl. Use a whisk or a fork to combine the mixture.
2. Next, add in the coconut oil and sprinkle in the peppermint essential oil, frankincense essential oil and sweet orange essential oil. Use a fork or a whisk to blend the mixture, taking care to break up any clumps that form from the oil.
3. Once the mixture is blended, begin misting it lightly with water while continuing to whisk it. Blend until the mixture is damp enough that when you form a ball with it in your hands it maintains it shape.
4. Firmly press the mixture into the molds that you are using.
5. Set the molds out on the counter and let them sit for 24 hours.
6. Remove the bath bombs from the mold and let them air dry for at least 24 hours.
7. Store them in a tightly covered container until ready to use.

To Use:
1. Place one large or two small bath bombs into warm bath water.
2. Soak for 15-20 minutes and enjoy.

Muscle Melt Bath Bombs

Materials:
1 cup baking soda
½ cup Epsom salt
½ cup citric acid
1 tablespoon avocado oil
10 drops eucalyptus essential oil
10 drops rosemary essential oil
5 drops peppermint essential oil
5 drops lavender essential oil
2 tablespoons dried mint leaves
Coffee grinder
Water for misting
Appropriate molds

Instructions:
1. Place the dried mint leaves in a coffee grinder and pulse until finely ground.
2. Combine the baking soda, Epson salt, citric acid and ground mint leaves in a large bowl. Use a whisk or a fork to combine the mixture.
3. Next, add in the avocado oil and sprinkle in the eucalyptus essential oil, rosemary essential oil, peppermint essential oil and lavender essential oil. Use a fork or a whisk to blend the mixture, taking care to break up any clumps that form from the oil.
4. Once the mixture is blended, begin misting it lightly with water while continuing to whisk it. Blend until the mixture is damp enough that when you form a ball with it in your hands it maintains it shape.
5. Firmly press the mixture into the molds that you are using.
6. Set the molds out on the counter and let them sit for 24 hours.

7. Remove the bath bombs from the mold and let them air dry for at least 24 hours.
8. Store them in a tightly covered container until ready to use.

To Use:
1. Place one large or two small bath bombs into warm bath water.
2. Soak for 15-20 minutes and enjoy.

Spiced Vanilla Mega Bombs

Materials:
2 ½ cup baking soda
1 ¼ cup citric acid
1 cup fine grain sea salt
1 tablespoon witch hazel
1 teaspoon ground cinnamon
10 drops sandalwood essential oil
10 drops vanilla absolute
Water for misting
Large mold

Instructions:
1. Combine the baking soda, citric acid, fine grain sea salt and cinnamon in a large bowl. Use a whisk or a fork to combine the mixture.
2. Next, add in the witch hazel and sprinkle in the sandalwood essential oil and vanilla absolute. Use a fork or a whisk to blend the mixture, taking care to break up any clumps that form from the oil.
3. Once the mixture is blended, begin misting it lightly with water while continuing to whisk it. Blend until the mixture is damp enough that when you form a ball with it in your hands it maintains it shape.
4. Firmly press the mixture into the large molds that you are using.
5. Set the molds out on the counter and let them sit for 24 hours.
6. Remove the bath bombs from the mold and let them air dry for at least 24-36 hours.
7. Store them in a tightly covered container until ready to use.

To Use:
1. Place one mega bomb in warm bath water.
2. Soak for 15-20 minutes and enjoy

Clarity and Wisdom Energizing Mega Bombs

Materials:
2 ½ cup baking soda
1 ¼ cup citric acid
1 cup fine grain sea salt
1 tablespoon witch hazel
10 drops clary sage essential oil
10 drops cypress essential oil
10 drops lemongrass essential oil
Water for misting
Large mold

Instructions:
1. Combine the baking soda, citric acid and fine grain sea salt in a large bowl. Use a whisk or a fork to combine the mixture.
2. Next, add in the witch hazel and sprinkle in the clary sage essential oil, cypress essential oil and lemongrass essential oil. Use a fork or a whisk to blend the mixture, taking care to break up any clumps that form from the oil.
3. Once the mixture is blended, begin misting it lightly with water while continuing to whisk it. Blend until the mixture is damp enough that when you form a ball with it in your hands it maintains it shape.
4. Firmly press the mixture into the large molds that you are using.
5. Set the molds out on the counter and let them sit for 24 hours.
6. Remove the bath bombs from the mold and let them air dry for at least 24-36 hours.
7. Store them in a tightly covered container until ready to use.

To Use:
1. Place one mega bomb in warm bath water.
2. Soak for 15-20 minutes and enjoy

Fatigue Busting Mega Bombs

Materials:
2 ½ cup baking soda
1 ¼ cup citric acid
1 cup fine grain sea salt
1 tablespoon witch hazel
1 teaspoon grapefruit zest
10 drops rosemary essential oil
10 drops jasmine essential oil
10 drops grapefruit essential oil
Water for misting
Large mold

Instructions:
1. Combine the baking soda, citric acid and fine grain sea salt in a large bowl. Use a whisk or a fork to combine the mixture.
2. Next, add in the witch hazel and sprinkle in the Rosemary essential oil, jasmine essential oil and grapefruit essential oil. Use a fork or a whisk to blend the mixture, taking care to break up any clumps that form from the oil.
3. Once the mixture is blended, begin misting it lightly with water while continuing to whisk it. Blend until the mixture is damp enough that when you form a ball with it in your hands it maintains it shape.
4. Firmly press the mixture into the large molds that you are using.
5. Set the molds out on the counter and let them sit for 24 hours.
6. Remove the bath bombs from the mold and let them air dry for at least 24-36 hours.
7. Store them in a tightly covered container until ready to use.

To Use:
1. Place one mega bomb in warm bath water.
2. Soak for 15-20 minutes and enjoy

Tropical Paradise Bath Bombs

Materials:
2 cups baking soda
1 ¼ cups cornstarch
1 cup citric acid
½ cup Epsom salt
1 tablespoon powdered coconut milk
1 tablespoon coconut oil, melted
10 drops geranium essential oil
10 drops sweet orange essential oil
5 drops cypress essential oil
Water for misting
Appropriate molds

Instructions:
1. Combine the baking soda, cornstarch, citric acid, Epsom salt, and powdered coconut milk in a large bowl. Use a whisk or a fork to combine the mixture.
2. Next, add the coconut oil and sprinkle in the geranium, sweet orange, and cypress essential oils. Use a fork or a whisk to blend the mixture, taking care to break up any clumps that form from the oil.
3. Once the mixture is blended, begin misting it lightly with water while continuing to whisk. Blend until the mixture is damp enough that when you form a ball with it in your hands it maintains its shape.
4. Firmly press the mixture into the molds you are using.
5. Set the molds out on the counter and let them sit for 24 hours.
6. Remove the bath bombs from the molds and let them air dry for at least 24 hours.
7. Store them in a tightly covered container until ready to use.

To Use:
1. Place one mega bomb in warm bath water.
2. Soak for 15-20 minutes and enjoy.

Coming Up Roses Bath Bombs

Materials:
2 cups baking soda
1 ¼ cups cornstarch
1 cup citric acid
½ cup Epsom salt
1 tablespoon dried rose petals, finely ground
1 tablespoon sweet almond oil
15 drops rose absolute
10 drops vanilla absolute
10 drops sweet orange essential oil
Water for misting
Appropriate molds

Instructions:
1. Combine the baking soda, cornstarch, citric acid, Epsom salt, and ground rose petals in a large bowl. Use a whisk or a fork to combine the mixture.
2. Next, add the sweet almond oil and sprinkle in the rose absolute, vanilla absolute and sweet orange essential oil. Use a fork or a whisk to blend the mixture, taking care to break up any clumps that form from the oil.
3. Once the mixture is blended, begin misting it lightly with water while continuing to whisk it. Blend until the mixture is damp enough that when you form a ball with it in your hands it maintains it shape.
4. Firmly press the mixture into the molds you are using.
5. Set the molds out on the counter and let them sit for 24 hours.
6. Remove the bath bombs from the molds and let them air dry for at least 24 hours.
7. Store them in a tightly covered container until ready to use.

To Use:
1. Place one mega bomb in warm bath water.
2. Soak for 15-20 minutes and enjoy.

Sweet Relief Bath Bombs

Materials:
2 cups baking soda
1 ¼ cups cornstarch
1 cup citric acid
½ cup Epsom salt
2 tablespoons dried chamomile flowers, finely ground
1 tablespoon sweet almond oil
10 drops chamomile essential oil
10 drops lavender essential oil
10 drops bergamot essential oil
Water for misting
Appropriate molds

Instructions:
1. Combine the baking soda, cornstarch, citric acid, Epsom salt, and ground chamomile in a large bowl. Use a whisk or a fork to combine the mixture.
2. Next, add the sweet almond oil and sprinkle in the chamomile, lavender, and bergamot essential oils. Use a fork or a whisk to blend the mixture, taking care to break up any clumps that form from the oil.
3. Once the mixture is blended, begin misting it lightly with water while continuing to whisk it. Blend until the mixture is damp enough that when you form a ball with it in your hands it maintains it shape.
4. Firmly press the mixture into the molds you are using.
5. Set the molds out on the counter and let them sit for 24 hours.
6. Remove the bath bombs from the molds and let them air dry for at least 24 hours.
7. Store them in a tightly covered container until ready to use.

To Use:
1. Place one mega bomb in warm bath water.
2. Soak for 15-20 minutes and enjoy.

Shower Gels and Body Cleansers

Homemade moisturizing bath gels are an incredible treat for your skin. So many of the bath gels you purchase are filled with ingredients you can't pronounce, are unnecessary – and in some cases, are actually bad for your skin. You can avoid all of that by making your own shower gels.

It has been said that making your own shower gels can be difficult. I think this is all a matter of perspective. If you are looking to replicate exactly the texture of manufactured shower gels, then yes, you are going to have your work cut out for you. However, you can create a cleanser that is emollient and thick with just a few ingredients and a very simple technique. Some of the shower gels shown here will have a somewhat milky color and consistency. This is natural and to be expected. One important thing to keep in mind is that when you make shower gels, you are adding water into the formula. Any time water is added, there is a potential for bacterial contamination. That is why antibacterial essential oils have been added to the formulas if they didn't already contain antiseptic ingredients. The amounts of these oils added is small and should not significantly affect the end result in terms of scent. You are always free to explore with other antibacterial essential oils as substitutions.

*Note: If you prefer the texture and sudsing capability of store bought shower gels, you can buy unscented shower gel bases from cosmetic supply companies and some natural food or craft stores. Just add extra moisturizing oils and scents.

Unscented Moisturizing Shower Gel

Materials:
¼ cup shea butter, melted
¼ cup avocado oil
2 teaspoons vitamin E oil
3 tablespoons vegetable glycerin
1 tablespoon xanthan gum
1 cup liquid castile soap
1 cup warm, distilled water
Container (clean and sterilized)
Immersion blender (or a whisk)

Instructions:
1. In a bowl, combine the melted shea butter, avocado oil, vitamin E oil, vegetable glycerin and xanthan gum. Stir gently and let the mixture sit for 5 minutes.
2. Using an immersion blender, blend the mixture until it begins to emulsify. (If you do not have an immersion blender, you can use a whisk.)
3. Add the castile soap and warm water. Whisk or quickly blend the ingredients for just a few seconds. Do not over mix and create suds.
4. Let the mixture settle for 1-2 minutes.
5. Pour the gel into an appropriate container, and store it in a cool, dry place.
6. For best results, make small batches that will be used within 14 days.

To Use:
1. Shake the container gently before use.
2. Apply the cleanser to a sponge or washcloth and cleanse the body.
3. Rinse with comfortably warm water and gently pat dry when finished.

Lavender Cocoa Butter Cleanser

Materials:
¼ cup cocoa butter, melted
¼ cup coconut oil
3 tablespoons vegetable glycerin
1 tablespoon xanthan gum
1 cup grated castile soap
1 cup warm, distilled water
30 drops lavender essential oil
Container (clean and sterile)
Immersion Blender (or whisk)

Instructions:
1. In a bowl, combine the melted cocoa butter, coconut oil, vegetable glycerin, and xanthan gum. Stir gently and let the mixture sit for 5 minutes.
2. Using an immersion blender (or a whisk if you do not have one), blend the mixture until it begins to emulsify.
3. Add the castile soap, warm water, and lavender essential oil. Whisk or quickly blend the ingredients for just a couple of seconds. Do not over mix and create suds.
4. Let the mixture settle for 1-2 minutes.
5. Pour the gel into an appropriate container, and store it in a cool, dry place.
6. For best results, make small batches that will be used within 14 days.

To Use:
1. Shake the container gently before use.
2. Apply the cleanser to a sponge or washcloth and cleanse the body.
3. Rinse with comfortably warm water and gently pat dry when finished.

Delicate Orange Blossom Milky Gel

Materials:
¼ cup shea butter, melted
¼ cup sweet almond oil
¼ cup powdered milk
3 tablespoons vegetable glycerin
1 tablespoon xanthan gum
1 cup liquid castile soap
1 cup warm, distilled water
¼ cup orange blossom water
10 drops neroli essential oil
5 drops grapefruit essential oil (as a preservative)
Container (clean and sterilized)
Immersion blender (or a whisk)

Instructions:
1. In a bowl, combine the melted shea butter, sweet almond oil, powdered milk, vegetable glycerin, and xanthan gum. Stir gently and let the mixture sit for 5 minutes.
2. Using an immersion blender (or a whisk if you do not have a blender), blend the mixture until it begins to emulsify.
3. Add the castile soap, warm water, orange blossom water, neroli essential oil, and grapefruit essential oil. Whisk or quickly blend the ingredients for just a couple of seconds. Do not over mix and create suds.
4. Let the mixture settle for 1-2 minutes.
5. Pour the gel into an appropriate container, and store it in a cool, dry place.
6. For best results, make small batches that will be used within 14 days.

To Use:
1. Shake the container gently before use.
2. Apply the cleanser to a sponge or washcloth and cleanse the body.
3. Rinse with comfortably warm water and gently pat dry when finished.

Rosemary and Tea Tree Aloe Shower Gel

Materials:
¼ cup shea butter, melted
¼ cup apricot oil
2 tablespoons aloe vera gel
3 tablespoons vegetable glycerin
1 tablespoon xanthan gum
1 cup grated castile soap
1 cup warm, distilled water
15 drops rosemary essential oil
15 drops tea tree essential oil
Container (clean and sterile)
Immersion blender (or a whisk)

Instructions:
1. In a bowl, combine the melted shea butter, apricot oil, aloe vera gel, vegetable glycerin, and xanthan gum. Stir gently and let the mixture sit for 5 minutes.
2. Using an immersion blender (or a whisk if you do not have one), blend the mixture until it begins to emulsify.
3. Add the castile soap, warm water, rosemary essential oil and tea tree essential oil. Whisk or quickly blend the ingredients for just a couple of seconds. Do not over mix and create suds.
4. Let the mixture settle for 1-2 minutes.
5. Pour the gel into an appropriate container, and store it in a cool, dry place.
6. For best results, make small batches that will be used within 14 days.

To Use:
1. Shake the container gently before use.
2. Apply the cleanser to a sponge or washcloth and cleanse the body.
3. Rinse with comfortably warm water and gently pat dry when finished.

Green Tea and Lemon Essence Shower Gel

Materials:
1 cup warm, distilled water
2 organic green tea teabags
¼ cup shea butter, melted
¼ cup sweet almond oil
1 tablespoon vitamin E oil
1 tablespoon witch hazel
3 tablespoons vegetable glycerin
1 tablespoon xanthan gum
1 cup grated castile soap
15 drops lemon essential oil
5 drops rosemary essential oil (as a preservative)
Container (clean and sterile)
Immersion blender (or a whisk)

Instructions:
1. Begin by heating the distilled water until it is steamy, and then steeping the tea bags until the temperature of the water cools to warm and not hot.
2. Remove the tea bags and strain any tea leaves from the brewed tea.
3. In a bowl, combine the melted shea butter, sweet almond oil oil, vitamin E oil, witch hazel, vegetable glycerin, and xanthan gum. Stir gently and let the mixture sit for 5 minutes.
4. Using an immersion blender (or a whisk if you do not have one), blend the mixture until it begins to emulsify.
5. Add the castile soap, brewed tea, lemon essential oil and rosemary essential oil. Whisk or quickly blend the ingredients for just a couple of seconds. Do not over mix and create suds.
6. Let the mixture settle for 1-2 minutes.

7. Pour the gel into an appropriate container, and store it in a cool, dry place.
8. For best results, make small batches that will be used within 14 days.

To Use:
1. Shake the container gently before use.
2. Apply the cleanser to a sponge or washcloth and cleanse the body.
3. Rinse with comfortably warm water and gently pat dry when finished.

Vanilla Milk and Honey Shower Gel

Materials:
1 cup liquid castile soap
1 cup coconut oil
1 cup local honey
¼ cups powdered coconut milk
15 drops vanilla absolute
5 drops rosemary essential oil (as a preservative)
Container (clean and sterile)
Immersion blender (or a whisk)

Instructions:
1. In a bowl, combine the liquid castile soap, coconut oil, honey, powdered coconut milk, vanilla absolute, and rosemary essential oil.
2. Let the mixture settle for 1-2 minutes.
3. Using an immersion blender (or a whisk if you do not have one), blend the mixture just long enough for it to emulsify. Try to avoid mixing it to the point that suds appear.
4. Pour the gel into an appropriate container, and store it in a cool, dry place.
5. For best results, make small batches that will be used within 14 days.

To Use:
1. Shake the container gently before use.
2. Apply the cleanser to a sponge or washcloth and cleanse the body.
3. Rinse with comfortably warm water and gently pat dry when finished.

Bees Knees Citrus Honey Wash

Materials:
1 cup liquid castile soap
¼ cup local honey
1 tablespoon vegetable glycerin
1 tablespoon vitamin E oil
1 tablespoon apricot kernel oil
10 drops sweet orange essential oil
5 drops grapefruit essential oil
5 drops lime essential oil
5 drops vanilla absolute
Container (clean and sterile)
Immersion blender (or a whisk)

Instructions:
1. In a bowl, combine the castile soap, local honey, vegetable glycerin, vitamin E oil, apricot kernel oil, sweet orange essential oil, grapefruit essential oil, lime essential oil, and vanilla absolute.
2. Let the mixture sit for 1-2 minutes.
3. Using an immersion blender (or a whisk if you do not have one), quickly blend the mixture just until it begins to emulsify. Try to avoid creating suds.
4. Pour the gel into an appropriate container, and store it in a cool, dry place.
5. For best results, make small batches that will be used within 14 days.

To Use:
1. Shake the container gently before use.
2. Apply the cleanser to a sponge or washcloth and cleanse the body.
3. Rinse with comfortably warm water and gently pat dry when finished.

Bubbly Baths

When it comes to quintessential elements of relaxation, few rate higher than an indulgent bubble bath. The experience can be even more luxurious when the bubbles that fill your tub are from a handcrafted formula, created to suit just the right mood. You might like your bubbles to be soothing and relaxing, exotic and floral, or energizing and mood lifting. Regardless of your preference, there is a bubble bath here to suit every personality and occasion. Homemade bubble baths also make excellent gifts that are always well received. It is important to note that homemade bubble baths include suds-producing ingredients like castile soap, vegetable glycerin, and certain oils. However, the type of bubble you get will be slightly different from your typical store bought bubble bath. The bubbles will be smaller and your bath water will feel more moisturizing. When you use homemade bubble baths, make sure that you pour the bath mixture directly under warm running water and agitate the water vigorously with your hand to produce the most and longest lasting bubbles.

Vanilla Rose Silky Bubble Bath

Materials:
1 cup sweet almond oil
½ cup liquid castile soap
½ cup local honey
15 drops rose absolute
10 drops vanilla absolute
Appropriate container

Instructions:
1. In a bowl, combine the sweet almond oil, liquid castile soap, and local honey.
2. Use a whisk to gently blend, taking care to not create extra suds.
3. Add the rose absolute and the vanilla absolute. Stir lightly with a spoon.
4. Transfer the bubble bath to an appropriate container.
5. Shake gently before using.

To Use:
1. Pour approximately ¼ cup of the bubble bath under warm running bath water.
2. Allow the bubbles to form as the bathtub fills with water.
3. Soak for 15-20 minutes and enjoy.

Rosemary Lavender Foaming Bath Tonic

Materials:
½ cup liquid castile soap
2 cups pure distilled water
½ cup coconut oil, melted
1 tablespoon witch hazel
20 drops lavender essential oil
15 drops rosemary essential oil
Appropriate container

Instructions:
1. In a bowl, gently blend together the liquid castile soap, the pure distilled water, and the coconut oil.
2. Once the mixture is blended, add the witch hazel, lavender essential oil, and rosemary essential oil.
3. Stir the mixture gently, taking care to not create extra suds.
4. Transfer the mixture to an appropriate container.
5. Shake gently before using.

To Use:
1. Pour approximately ¼ cup of the bubble bath under warm running bath water.
2. Allow the bubbles to form as the bathtub fills with water.
3. Soak for 15-20 minutes and enjoy.

Extra Foamy Vanilla Nutmeg Bubble Bath

Materials:
2 cups liquid castile soap
½ cup vegetable glycerin
¼ cup coconut oil, melted
20 drops vanilla absolute
5 drops sandalwood essential oil
½ teaspoon freshly ground nutmeg
Appropriate container

Instructions:
1. In a bowl, combine the liquid castile soap, vegetable glycerin, and coconut oil.
2. Use a whisk to gently blend the mixture.
3. Next, add the vanilla absolute, sandalwood essential oil, and freshly ground nutmeg.
4. Stir gently with a spoon just enough to incorporate the oils and nutmeg. Take care to not create extra suds while mixing.
5. Transfer the bubble bath to an appropriate container.
6. Shake gently before using.

To Use:
1. Pour approximately ¼ cup of the bubble bath under warm running bath water.
2. Allow the bubbles to form as the bathtub fills with water.
3. Soak for 15-20 minutes and enjoy.

Lemon Eucalyptus Bubbly Honey Bath

Materials:
1 cup liquid castile soap
1 cup sweet almond oil
½ cup local honey
½ cup vegetable glycerin
15 drops lemon essential oil
15 drops eucalyptus essential oil
Appropriate container

Instructions:
1. In a bowl, combine the liquid castile soap, sweet almond oil, local honey, and vegetable glycerin. Use a whisk to gently combine the ingredients.
2. Next, add the lemon essential oil and the eucalyptus essential oil. Stir gently with a whisk or a spoon to incorporate the oils. Take care to nor produce extra suds while mixing.
3. Transfer the bubbly bath to an appropriate container.
4. Shake gently before using.

To Use:
1. Pour approximately ¼ cup of the bubble bath under warm running bath water.
2. Allow the bubbles to form as the bathtub fills with water.
3. Soak for 15-20 minutes and enjoy.

Sniffles Be Gone Bath Suds

Materials:
2 cups liquid castile soap
1 cup vegetable glycerin
¼ cup evening primrose oil
15 drops thyme essential oil
10 drops rosemary essential oil
10 drops peppermint essential oil
Fresh rosemary sprig
Appropriate container

Instructions:
1. In a bowl, combine the liquid castile soap, vegetable glycerin, and the evening primrose oil. Mix gently with a whisk or spoon.
2. Add the thyme, rosemary, and peppermint essential oils. Stir gently to incorporate the oils, taking care to not create extra suds while mixing.
3. Place the rosemary sprig in the container you plan to use.
4. Carefully pour the bubble bath into the container.
5. Shake gently before using.

To Use:
1. Pour approximately ¼ cup of the bubble bath under warm running bath water.
2. Allow the bubbles to form as the bathtub fills with water.
3. Soak for 15-20 minutes and enjoy.

Jasmine Scented Bubbly

Materials:
1 cup liquid castile soap
1 cup barely warm brewed green tea
½ cup vegetable glycerin
¼ cup coconut oil
20 drops jasmine essential oil
10 drops vanilla absolute
5 drops neroli essential oil
Appropriate container

Instructions:
1. In a bowl, combine the liquid castile soap, warm brewed green tea, vegetable glycerin, and coconut oil.
2. Use a whisk or a spoon to gently combine the ingredients.
3. Next, add the jasmine essential oil, vanilla absolute, and neroli essential oil.
4. Mix gently until the essential oils are incorporated, taking care not to create extra suds while mixing.
5. Pour the bubble bath into an appropriate container.
6. Shake gently before using.

To Use:
1. Pour approximately ¼ cup of the bubble bath under warm running bath water.
2. Allow the bubbles to form as the bathtub fills with water.
3. Soak for 15-20 minutes and enjoy.

Just For Him Relaxing Bubble Bath

Materials:
1 cup liquid castile soap
1 cup strong brewed black tea
½ cup vegetable glycerin
¼ cup avocado oil
15 drops sandalwood essential oil
10 drops cypress essential oil
5 drops sweet rosemary essential oil
2-3 drops clove essential oil (do not use more than this as it can be irritating to the skin in more concentrated amounts)

Instructions:
1. In a bowl, combine the liquid castile soap, strong brewed black tea, vegetable glycerin, and avocado oil. Mix gently using a whisk or spoon.
2. Add the sandalwood, cypress, rosemary, and clove essential oils.
3. Stir gently, just until the essential oils are incorporated. Take care not to create excess suds while mixing.
4. Transfer the bubble bath to an appropriate container.
5. Shake gently before using.

To Use:
1. Pour approximately ¼ cup of the bubble bath under warm running bath water.
2. Allow the bubbles to form as the bathtub fills with water.
3. Soak for 15-20 minutes and enjoy.

Baby Your Baby Gentle Bubble Bath

Materials:
2 cups liquid castile soap
½ cup vegetable glycerin
¼ cup sweet almond oil
2 tablespoons coconut oil, melted
10 drops lavender essential oil
10 drops chamomile essential oil
5 drops rose absolute
Appropriate container

Instructions:
1. In a bowl, combine the liquid castile soap, vegetable glycerin, sweet almond oil, and coconut oil. Use a whisk or a spoon to gently blend the ingredients together.
2. Add the lavender essential oil, chamomile essential oil, and rose absolute.
3. Gently stir just until the oils are incorporated, taking care not to create extra suds while mixing.
4. Pour the bubble bath into an appropriate container.
5. Shake gently before using.

To Use:
1. Pour approximately ¼ cup of the bubble bath under warm running bath water.
2. Allow the bubbles to form as the bathtub fills with water.
3. Soak for 15-20 minutes and enjoy.

Energizing Citrus Bubbly

Materials:
1 cup liquid castile soap
½ cup sweet almond oil
½ cup local honey
½ cup vegetable glycerin
10 drops tangerine essential oil
10 drops lemongrass essential oil
10 drops peppermint essential oil
5 drops jasmine essential oil
Appropriate container

Instructions:
1. In a bowl, combine the liquid castile soap, sweet almond oil, local honey, and vegetable glycerin. Use a whisk or a spoon to blend gently.
2. Next, add the tangerine, lemongrass, peppermint, and jasmine essential oils.
3. Gently blend just until the oils are incorporated, taking care not to create excess suds while mixing.
4. Pour the bubble bath into an appropriate container.
5. Shake gently before using.

To Use:
1. Pour approximately ¼ cup of the bubble bath under warm running bath water.
2. Allow the bubbles to form as the bathtub fills with water.
3. Soak for 15-20 minutes and enjoy.

Bath Teas

One of the simplest and most beautiful ways of enhancing your bath water is by creating bath teas from your favorite dried herbs and flowers. The combinations are endless and each creation can be a transformative experience. Bath teas also make beautiful gifts. You can place them in traditional tea tins, or package them into individual tea bags. You can even gift them with a large tea strainer. The amount of dried tea you place in your bath will be significantly more than what you might use in a cup of tea. You can use two to three standard size tea strainers, purchase extra-large tea bags, or craft your own tea bags out of a porous natural fabric, such as muslin. You can also sprinkle the bath teas straight into the water; the only downside to this is that it can be a little messy to clean up when you are finished.

Ultra Soothing Chamomile Lavender Bath Tea

Materials:
1 cup dried lavender flowers
1 cup dried chamomile flowers
½ cup oatmeal
10 drops lavender essential oil
10 drops chamomile essential oil
Airtight container for storage
Tea bag or tea strainer, if using

Instructions:
1. In a large bowl, combine the dried lavender flowers, dried chamomile flowers, and the oatmeal.
2. Sprinkle the lavender essential oil and chamomile essential oil over the dried mixture and stir to blend them in.
3. Transfer the tea to an airtight container until ready to use or gift.

To Use:
1. Add approximately ¼–½ cup of the bath tea to a large empty tea bag, and put it in warm bath water. You can avoid the straining device and sprinkle the tea directly into the bath water if desired.
2. Soak for 15-20 minutes and enjoy.

Antioxidant Bath Tea

Materials:
1 ½ cups green tea
½ cup white tea
½ cup Epsom salt
15 drops bergamot essential oil
Airtight container for storage
Tea bag or tea strainer, if using

Instructions:
1. In a large bowl, combine the green tea, white tea, and Epsom salt.
2. Sprinkle the bergamot essential oil over the tea mixture and stir to blend in the oil.
3. Transfer to an airtight container until ready to use or gift.

To Use:
1. Add approximately ¼–½ cup of the bath tea to a large empty tea bag, and place it in warm bath water. Avoid the straining device and sprinkle the tea directly into the bath water if desired.
2. Soak for 15-20 minutes and enjoy.

Chai Bath Tea

Materials:
1 cup dry chai tea blend
1 cup green tea
½ cup Epsom salt
½ teaspoon ground cinnamon
1 tablespoon whole cloves
1 teaspoon orange zest
10 drops vanilla absolute
5 drops sweet orange essential oil
Airtight container
Tea bag or tea strainer, if using.

Instructions:
1. In a large bowl, combine the chai tea blend, green tea, Epsom salt, ground cinnamon, whole cloves, and orange zest.
2. Sprinkle the vanilla absolute and sweet orange essential oil over the tea mixture and stir to blend in the oils.
3. Transfer to an airtight container until ready to use or gift.

To Use:
1. Add approximately ¼–½ cup of the bath tea to a large empty tea bag, and drop it into warm bath water. Avoid the straining device and sprinkle the tea directly into the bath water if desired.
2. Soak for 15-20 minutes and enjoy.

Sniffle Relief Bath Tea

Materials:
1 cup green tea
½ cup Epsom salt
½ cup dried peppermint leaves
2 tablespoons dried rosemary
10 drops eucalyptus essential oil
10 drops rosemary essential oil
5 drops peppermint essential oil
5 drops lemon essential oil
Airtight container
Tea bag or tea strainer, if using

Instructions:
1. In a large bowl, combine the green tea, Epsom salt, dried peppermint leaves, and dried rosemary.
2. Sprinkle the eucalyptus, rosemary, peppermint, and lemon essential oils over the tea mixture. Stir to blend in the oils.
3. Transfer the tea to an airtight container until ready to use or gift.

To Use:
1. Add approximately ¼–½ cup of the bath tea to a large empty tea bag, and add it to warm bath water. Avoid the straining device and sprinkle the tea directly into the bath water if desired.
2. Soak for 15-20 minutes and enjoy.

Cypress Lime Bath Tea

Materials:
1 ½ cups black tea
½ cup Epsom salt
10 drops cypress essential oil
5 drops cedar essential oil
5 drops lime essential oil
Airtight container
Tea bag or tea strainer, if using

Instructions:
1. Combine the black tea and Epsom salt in a large bowl.
2. Sprinkle the cypress, cedar, and lime essential oils over the tea mixture. Stir until the oils are blended in.
3. Transfer the tea to an airtight container until ready to use or gift.

To Use:
1. Add approximately ¼–½ cup of the bath tea to a large empty tea bag, and drop it into warm bath water. Avoid the straining device and sprinkle the tea directly into the bath water if desired.
2. Soak for 15-20 minutes and enjoy.

Brighten Up Buttercup Bath Tea

Materials:
1 cup dried buttercup (or other preferred flower) petals
1 cup hibiscus tea
½ cup Epsom salt
10 drops jasmine essential oil
5 drops bergamot essential oil
5 drops geranium essential oil
5 drops lemon essential oil
Airtight container
Tea bag or tea strainer, if using

Instructions:
1. Combine the buttercup petals, hibiscus tea, and Epsom salt in a large bowl.
2. Sprinkle the jasmine, bergamot, geranium, and lemon essential oils over the tea mixture. Stir to blend in the oils.
3. Transfer the tea to an airtight container until ready to use or gift.

To Use:
1. Add approximately ¼–½ cup of the bath tea to a large empty tea bag, and add it to warm bath water. Avoid the straining device and sprinkle the tea directly into the bath water if desired.
2. Soak for 15-20 minutes and enjoy.

Hop To It Bath Tea

Materials:
1 ½ cups green tea
½ cup Epsom salt
¼ cup oatmeal
2 tablespoons Cascadia hops
10 drops bergamot essential oil
10 drops grapefruit essential oil
5 drops lavender essential oil

Instructions:
1. Combine the green tea, Epsom salt, oatmeal, and Cascadia hops in a large bowl.
2. Sprinkle the bergamot, grapefruit, and lavender essential oils over the tea mixture. Stir until the oils are blended.
3. Transfer the tea to an airtight container until ready to use or gift.

To Use:
1. Add approximately ¼–½ cup of the bath tea to a large empty tea bag, and add it to warm bath water. Avoid the straining device and sprinkle the tea directly into the bath water if desired.
2. Soak for 15-20 minutes and enjoy.

Body Scrubs and Suds

There is no question that soaking in a healing natural bath is a luxurious experience. However, we can't neglect to include some recipes for indulgent body scrubs and cleansers that treat your skin with pure decadence. Keep in mind that even though the individual ingredients of these recipes are shelf stable, you can preserve the quality and shelf life of the finished products by keeping them in the refrigerator, or at least making sure they are stored away from heat and excess moisture.

Smooth as Silk Body Scrub

Materials:

½ cup sweet almond oil
¼ cup avocado oil
1 tablespoon vitamin E
1 tablespoon powdered honey
15 drops lavender essential oil
1 cup sea salt
Glass container with airtight lid

Instructions:

1. In a large bowl, combine the sweet almond oil, avocado oil, vitamin E, powdered honey, and lavender essential oil.
2. Using a whisk or a wooden spoon, slowly stir the sea salt into the oil mixture until a thick paste has formed.
3. Transfer the body scrub to a glass container with an airtight lid.
4. Store in a cool, dry place for at least 3-4 days before using.

To Use:

1. Using your fingertips or a small beauty spatula, scoop out a generous portion of the body scrub and rub it gently over your body, working up towards your heart.
2. Rinse with comfortably warm water and gently pat dry.

Honey Almond Brown Sugar Scrub

Materials:
1 ½ cups brown sugar
½ cup ground almonds
1 cup sweet almond oil
2 tablespoons local honey
10 drops vanilla absolute
5 drops lemon essential oil
Airtight container

Instructions:
1. Combine the brown sugar and ground almonds in one bowl.
2. In a separate bowl, combine the sweet almond oil, local honey, vanilla absolute, and lemon essential oil.
3. Using a whisk or a wooden spoon, slowly add the brown sugar mixture into the oil mixture, stirring until a thick paste forms.
4. Transfer the body scrub to an airtight container and store it in a cool, dry place for at least 3-4 days before using.

To Use:
1. Using your fingertips or a small beauty spatula, scoop out a generous portion of the body scrub and rub it gently over your body, working up towards your heart.
2. Rinse with comfortably warm water and gently pat dry.

Masculine Dead Sea Scrub

Materials:
1 cup sweet almond oil
10 drops cypress essential oil
10 drops vetiver essential oil
5 drops tea tree essential oil
2 cups Dead Sea salt
Airtight container

Instructions:
1. In a bowl, combine the sweet almond oil with the cypress, vetiver, and tea tree essential oils. Stir gently.
2. Slowly add the Dead Sea salt into the oil mixture, stirring until a thick paste forms.
3. Transfer the body scrub to an airtight container.
4. Store in a cool, dry place for at least 3-4 days before using.

To Use:
1. Using your fingertips or a small beauty spatula, scoop out a generous portion of the body scrub and rub it gently over your body, working up towards your heart.
2. Rinse with comfortably warm water and gently pat dry.

Skin Brightening Coffee Scrub

Materials:
1 cup brown sugar
1 cup ground coffee
¼ cup jojoba oil
½ cup coconut oil, melted
15 drops orange essential oil
Airtight container

Instructions:
1. Combine the brown sugar and ground coffee in one bowl.
2. In a separate bowl, combine the jojoba oil, coconut oil, and orange essential oil.
3. Using a whisk or a wooden spoon, slowly add the dry mixture to the oils. Stir until a thick paste forms.
4. Transfer the body scrub to an airtight container.
5. Store in a cool, dry place for 3-4 days before using.

To Use:
1. Using your fingertips or a small beauty spatula, scoop out a generous portion of the body scrub and rub it gently over your body, working up towards your heart.
2. Rinse with comfortably warm water and gently pat dry.

Rosemary Lemon Salt Scrub

Materials:
1 cup coarse grain salt
2 tablespoons dried rosemary, chopped
1 tablespoon lemon zest
½ cup pure olive oil
5 drops rosemary essential oil
5 drops lemon essential oil
Air tight container

Instructions:
1. In a bowl, combine the salt, rosemary, and lemon zest.
2. In a separate bowl, combine the olive oil with the rosemary and lemon essential oils.
3. Using a whisk or a wooden spoon, slowly add the salt mixture into the oil mixture, and stir until a thick paste forms.
4. Transfer the mixture to an airtight container.
5. Store in a cool, dry place for 3-4 days before using.

To Use:
1. Using your fingertips or a small beauty spatula, scoop out a generous portion of the body scrub and rub it gently over your body, working up towards your heart.
2. Rinse with comfortably warm water and gently pat dry.

Luscious Lemon Lime Sugar Scrub

Materials:
1 cup white sugar
1 teaspoon lemon zest
1 teaspoon lime zest
½ cup sweet almond oil
1 tablespoon fresh lemon juice
10 drops lime essential oil
5 drops bergamot essential oil
5 drops vanilla absolute
Airtight container

Instructions:
1. Combine the white sugar with the lemon zest and lime zest in a bowl.
2. In a separate large bowl, combine the sweet almond oil, lemon juice, lime essential oil, bergamot essential oil, and vanilla absolute.
3. Using a whisk or a wooden spoon, slowly add the sugar mixture to the oils. Blend until a thick paste forms.
4. Transfer the scrub to an airtight container.
5. Store in a cool, dry place for 3-4 days before using.

To Use:
1. Using your fingertips or a small beauty spatula, scoop out a generous portion of the body scrub and rub it gently over your body, working up towards your heart.
2. Rinse with comfortably warm water and gently pat dry.

Sweet Peppermint Scrub

Materials:
1 cup white sugar
1 tablespoon dried mint leaves, ground
½ cup coconut oil, melted
10 drops peppermint essential oil
10 drops spearmint essential oil
5 drops vanilla absolute
Airtight container

Instructions:
1. Combine the white sugar with the dried mint leaves in a bowl.
2. In a separate large bowl, combine the coconut oil, peppermint essential oil, spearmint essential oil, and the vanilla absolute.
3. Using a whisk or a wooden spoon, slowly add the sugar mixture to the oils. Blend until a thick paste forms.
4. Transfer the mixture to an airtight container.
5. Store in a cool, dry place for 3-4 days before using.

To Use:
1. Using your fingertips or a small beauty spatula, scoop out a generous portion of the body scrub and rub it gently over your body, working up towards your heart.
2. Rinse with comfortably warm water and gently pat dry.

Cedar Rose Moisturizing Body Wash

Materials:
1 cup liquid castile soap
½ cup coconut oil, melted
½ cup local honey
2 teaspoons vitamin E oil
15 drops cedar essential oil
20 drops rose absolute
Glass container with a tight fitting lid
Large glass measuring cup

Instructions:
1. Place the liquid castile soap in a large glass measuring cup.
2. Slowly add the coconut oil, local honey, vitamin E oil, cedar essential oil, and rose absolute. Stir gently with a spoon until combined. Do not whisk or stir too aggressively or bubbles may form.
3. Slowly transfer the wash to a glass container and seal it tightly.
4. Store in a cool, dry place.

To Use:
1. Apply the wash to a bath sponge or washcloth and add water to create suds.
2. Wash as desired and rinse with comfortably warm water. Pat dry gently when you are finished.

Tea Tree and Honey Restorative Body Wash

Materials:

1 cup liquid castile soap
¾ cup local honey
½ cup pure olive oil
20 drops tea tree essential oil
Glass container with a tight fitting lid
Large glass measuring cup

Instructions:
1. Pour the liquid castile soap into the measuring cup.
2. Slowly add the local honey, olive oil, and tea tree essential oil. Stir the mixture slowly with a spoon. Avoid whisking or aggressively mixing the liquid as bubbles may result.
3. Slowly pour the wash into the glass container and seal it tightly.
4. Store in a cool, dry place.

To Use:
1. Apply the wash to a bath sponge or washcloth and add water to create suds.
2. Wash as desired and rinse with comfortably warm water. Pat dry gently when you are finished.

Milky Chamomile Wash

Materials:
1 cup liquid castile soap
½ cup local honey
½ cup pure olive oil
¼ cup powdered milk
25 drops chamomile essential oil
Glass container with a tight fitting lid
Large glass measuring cup

Instructions:
1. Place the liquid castile soap in a large glass measuring cup.
2. Slowly add the powdered local honey, pure olive oil, powdered milk, and chamomile essential oil. Stir gently using a spoon. Do not whisk or stir aggressively or bubbles may form.
3. Slowly transfer the wash to a glass container and seal it tightly.
4. Store in a cool, dry place.

To Use:
1. Apply the wash to a bath sponge or washcloth and add water to create suds.
2. Wash as desired and rinse with comfortably warm water. Pat dry gently when you are finished.

Conclusion

Once you realize how incredibly easy it is to make homemade bath products you will never reach for a manufactured brand again. Homemade products provide the absolute best in therapeutic value and luxury. I hope you have discovered this for yourself as you have worked your way through this book, crafting natural bath products for yourself and for others.

When we bathe, we are at one of our most basic states. It is the point where we shed the past and cleanse ourselves to refresh and renew our spirit. Not every shower or bath needs to feel like a ritual, but the wonderful truth is that it can be. There is no reason to not treat yourself, and those you create these bath products for, to pure, natural bath time treats. Enjoy!

More Books from Josephine Simon